The Art

of the

Q

∫

The Art of the Q

Build Your Business with Questions

Charlie Van Hecke

∫

SalesTrainer4U, Charlottesville, VA

.

Copyright © 2014 by Charlie Van Hecke.

For information, on reprints, permissions, etc., please contact the author at charlievanhecke@gmail.com.

Published by SalesTrainer4U, 536 Pantops Center, Suite 210, Charlottesville, VA 22911 USA. First edition.

ISBN 978-1-4996411-6-5

Printed by CreateSpace, Charleston, SC.

Designed by Chenille Books, Charlottesville, VA.

EBOOK IS AVAILABLE

Purchase the digital edition of **The Art of the Q** – available wherever ebooks are sold.

∫

Contents

∫

Author's Note

You may be asking, "Why Q?"

Here's how I answer your question, in basic terms:

Asking questions builds better relationships and helps you achieve closure.

The simple gesture of interaction suggests that you want to understand and listen.

When you have better relationships, the quality of your life improves.

When these are in place, your professional life and career will blossom.

When you read **The Art of the Q** you will learn to eliminate bad behaviors and insert new success habits.

So, do YOU want to Q?

— *Charlie Van Hecke*

Charlottesville, VA

INTRODUCTION

The Art of the Q

Do You Q? If you do, you'll save time and make more money.

Q stands for Questions. And, as you'll see, questions and qualification are closely linked.

A sequence of questions becomes the process of Qualification.

Are you in the business of people? Questioning helps us interact and understand other people so we can satisfy the needs and wants of our customers. This leads to sales success for each and every business-person who reads, applies, and practices the art of qualification. If you think, "But I'm not in sales," take a moment to consider that with me. Read through this introduction, and ask yourself how much of it actually applies to your own career and life. These days, I believe, we're all in sales, whether selling ideas or methods or solutions or widgets.

Our **questioning sequences** will help you gather information in more strategic and persuasive ways. **The Art of the Q** begins with a review of many tips and skills that help you return to success habits, or remind you to get back to the basics, like listening. The skills, methods, and practical information-gathering tools in **The Art of the Q** will keep you from making common mistakes.

Next, the intermediate section will give lots of **probing examples** to help you become a better communicator. We illustrate this skill with a story about a traffic accident where police, insurance, legal, and medical professionals each gather information to do their jobs. This should help ALL business people take a look at questions from a different perspective. Once we establish the effectiveness of sequencing questions, we arrive at the star of our experience: The **SCAN** Method.

The reader can expect powerful discovery skills with the **SCAN** Method, which was inspired by a medical sequence in use by doctors. It helps people **probe and discover** hidden needs and wants with **persuasive** structure and purpose. Emphasizing the importance of relationship-building, the **SCAN** Method transforms a sales person from order-taker to game-changer. It also eliminates a lot of obstacles later in the sales process by building an agenda based on the needs of the buyer.

An entire section examines presentations, only as they relate to the **confirmation of need**. You'll find ways to pique interest by tailoring presentations around needs. An easy communication technique follows an **NFAB-Check** outline, to help you flow from needs discovery to presentation in an effortless and persuasive manner.

Many of my students develop an appreciation for the basics after getting into **buyer counseling**. Read this section carefully. We focus on counseling and closing, using **deeper qualification** to support the buyer in the making of **late stage decisions**. Through call objectives and next-step selling, business people can advance the sale using **trial closes** and **next-step questions without fear of being pushy or rude**. This section highlights a case study using a sequence of questions that includes a trial close.

Case Studies and Examples

Sales people come in all shapes and sizes. Perhaps the most important sales person of all is the one that does not realize that they are in sales: **Business Owners!** We will examine case studies for Business to Business (B2B) as well as Business to Consumer (B2C) sales.

We will visit professionals in case studies to learn lessons about the role of questions in communication. We will also highlight the internal qualities of super communicators. By combining skills, qualities, and methods, readers can expect to improve their communication abilities. (Keep reading for a complete list of the case studies and stories included in this book.)

What's in It for You?

What's in this for you? The abilities **to ask questions** and **to qualify** are two core competencies. Whether you target businesses or consumers in your work, you need these skills. Yes, **Q stands for Questions**; **multiple questions become the process of Qualifi-**

cation. Questions and qualification sequence queries are skills that every businessperson needs. In the end, **we are all in sales**.

Questions will help you **differentiate** your products and **get a higher price** by getting buyers to become aware of their needs and wants.

Qualification helps **save you time** by identifying buyers who will say yes to you.

Questions help you identify and remove obstacles.

Qualification helps you **prioritize real buyers** who can afford your solutions.

You will save time and make more money.

So...Do You Ask Questions Now?

You probably do Q.

And you probably want to get better to become even more awesome!

Business Owners Are in Sales!

The Varietals of sales are not limited to big companies; you can contrast them by industries as well. Just in the field of construction, you could find many different types of sales people. For instance, if you are going to renovate a house, you might talk to:

Plumbers. Electricians. Roofers. Flooring Installers. Carpeting Installers. Window Replacement Specialists. House Painters.

Oh, you don't think of those folks as sales people? Watch the next time an estimator visits. They ask questions, submit estimates on the repair, and overcome objections. They stress the backlog and scarcity of labor, and even close. Yes, Yes, Yes, they are sales people.

A plumber once came to one of my seminars and sat in the back row. To draw him into the discussion, I asked him:

Can you describe your estimate process?

Does everyone always say yes?

The plumber explained to the group that his customers are very frugal and some folks only fix the most urgent issues.

"Why is that?" I asked.

The plumber replied, "Because my customers do not realize that it will cost them more money in the long term to fix things right!"

From there, we went into discussions about how questions can get buyers to become aware of the consequences of their decisions. The plumber literally stood up and **moved to the front of the class** to learn more. **Everyone** faces price objections with frugal customers.

We will provide examples of consequence questions and devote an entire chapter to counseling. My belief is that these questions will not only help you make more money, they will help keep your customer base satisfied.

Many professionals may not know (or admit) their internal sales identity. In reality, most know it but do not want to be VIEWED as sales people. They want to be seen as consultants – who are concerned only with the needs of their customers.

In this book's chapter, **Closing the Sale**, we address **next-step selling to advance the sale**. Many sales managers are afraid that acting like consultants will make their team soft or less aggressive. In fact, though, these skills give you the ability to be both task oriented AND aware of relationships.

These are behavior improvements. Could the key be between our ears?

THE INTERNAL QUALITIES OF SUPER COMMUNICATORS

You will learn about and **unlock your internal qualities** to become a **super communicator**! Business people who work on their internal traits find the keys to success despite industry change or recession. My hope in the short term is that you make **more money with less work**. In the long term, I believe this book can **transform your career** and help you build a more satisfied and loyal customer base. As a bonus, it is likely to help communication in all of your relationships, but remember, this is a book about communication in your professional world.

All experts agree we should become better listeners. You may be a house painter or a dentist. You may be a professional sales person or the owner of a carpet store. The number one skill you need is communication, and listening is the key. What skill facilitates listening? **The art and science of questioning promotes better listening**.

It starts with the research you do before you make contact, and develops over the phone, in emails, texts, and face-to-face communications. Strategic sales people and business owners who succeed **ask questions**. Some questions are very basic.

Smart business people develop structure in their information gathering tools to find out the needs, wants, preferences, and patterns of their customers.

Becoming an expert about your customers before you suggest a solution is often the marginal difference between winning and losing. It is a **competitive edge** that makes the difference.

The Art of the Q will start with easy questions and move on to intermediate sequences with examples and case studies. We will finish with a method of discovery that will help you when you're deep into the buying process. Scripting exercises along the way will promote the transfer of learning from these pages into your daily conversations.

In **The Art of the Q**, stories stripped from real life will provide examples. Just remember that, at a very basic level, questions can help all business people. I recently met a contractor who built a business around two basic questions. I have selected this case study first because this businessperson is doing well **despite an economic downturn**.

Case Study: The House Painter

A local networking group sponsors an exhibition for new businesses. Each business owner has a booth where visitors can roam around the tables and shop. A man walks up to me and hands me a business card.

He asks two questions:

Do you need a painter?

Are there any sections of your house – inside or out that need painting?

After this discussion, I ask a few questions of my own:

How do you promote this business?

How busy are you?

How do you get leads?

The painter explains that he is very busy and gets all of his business by word of mouth. Instead of watching television, he goes to local events, hands out business cards, and asks the same two questions over and over again.

Do you need a painter?

Are there any sections of your house – inside or out – that need painting?

Then, he does an excellent job and asks his customers for referrals.

He repeats this process all the time. The painter is booked every week. In his spare time (at least one hour a day), he hands out business cards and asks questions. No Facebook. No Yellow Pages. No Website. No Literature. No marketing of any kind. The painter uses the same process every time. He asks two questions and hands out business cards. After he paints for you, he gets referrals. Repeat process.

Boring? To some people, it may appear to be repetitive. But this painter eliminates time wasters, and is efficient in lead generation.

Please visit our website at *www.salestrainer4u.com/services.html* to learn about getting new business utilizing the **Target10toWin!** Program.

CASE STUDIES AND STORIES IN **The Art of the Q**

At every stage of **The Art of the Q** we will provide real-life examples so you can apply these skills to your situation. Some may seem basic – but we will move into intermediate topics like questioning sequences. We'll review internal qualities and positive attitudes relating to communication. Questions – and specifically qualification – can put money in your pocket and save you hours of effort.

These subjects are prerequisites (building blocks) for advanced skills like the **SCAN** Method. The added layers of counseling and closing **help you stay task oriented while preserving relationships**.

I passionately believe that if you read, absorb, and apply **The Art of the Q** then YOU will learn to become more efficient and successful in business, sales, and life.

CVH

1

BASIC COMMUNICATION SKILLS THAT BUILD RELATIONSHIPS

I recently overheard my wife say, "Enough about me. Tell me about you!"

This gentle transition represents a skill we can label **breaking the ice**. The conversation had begun with chitchat – light, non-threatening discussion. Not all people enjoy small talk, but it often helps warm up a relationship. My wife believes that **relationships are everything in business**. Small talk is just one way to **build rapport**.

Building Rapport

When you initiate a conversation, be sure to make eye contact and smile. The goal is to connect and establish a common bond so that you can communicate effectively. A proven way to build rapport is to simply thank people for their time. **Use this with**

very busy decision makers when you need to get to the point right away. Obviously, it is easier to establish rapport when you are in a live, face-to-face environment.

If you are on a phone call or Web call (Skype, Face-time, or Online Meeting), then it is more challenging to connect with an audience. We will address this later in a case study called "Wows, Webinars, and Whoops!"

Whether you are live or online, **small talk is a time-tested way to break the ice**. Chatting briefly about the weather, a company or personal achievement, or common allegiances (alma maters, sports teams) are all ways that great communicators establish and build rapport. Humor is also fantastic, if it is tasteful and appropriate.

Be careful, though, giving compliments unless the comment is based on research and is extremely **genuine**. You will want to open with a couple of questions, and then be ready to move quickly into a relevant conversation. We will also address how to converse with **task oriented** decision makers.

Questions for Great Openings

If a meeting or an appointment has been set, then you know there is a need or want that requires satisfaction. When buyers call and ask you to come to their home or office, they have a reason. Then, when you start the meeting, that reason should be your first discussion point.

Read the example below and notice how efficiently the businessperson builds rapport, brings up the topic of interest, and begins the discovery process.

Case Study: Home Improvement

"Thank you for meeting with me today. On the phone last week, you said you had some concerns **about your kitchen and bathrooms**. According to a recent report, kitchen and bathroom improvements are the **top two ways to increase the value of your home**. I'd like to ask you some questions about your home improvement goals."

What are you hoping to accomplish?

Are there budget parameters or is the sky the limit? (Laugh)

This example illustrates how to 1) build rapport, 2) remind the buyer of key motivators, and 3) ask some good open-ended questions to get the conversation started. Yes, the best sales people use humor and it usually (but not always) helps to loosen folks up. Each businessperson has to make up his or her mind on humor depending on the industry and clientele.

Either way, you get the point and now have a script that you can apply in your own sales efforts. When you create a script, you write down what you are going to ask and say on a sales call. Yes, actors and actresses have scripts. They practice their lines until it is natural.

Sales people who want to move to the next level should also script and practice their questions! These business professionals find that you can focus on both task and relationship.

Why Use the Open-Ended Q?

Open-ended questions are valuable in the communication process because they 1) encourage the buyers to talk about themselves, and 2) provide an opportunity to get valuable information.

Asking questions is similar to playing tennis. When someone hits the tennis ball, you want to hit the ball back over the net and have a volley. Do the same in conversation. Ask a question and let the other person talk. People who are hyper-motivated to engage other people like to understand their customers.

You are not trying to smash the ball or win the volley! You are hoping to have a relevant interaction with low tension. Small exchanges lead to long-term dialogue and profitable relationships.

As a general rule (not an absolute), pick one or two questions to initiate a sales call, and then listen carefully to your buyer's answers.

Here is an example of what you might say to start a conversation with a buyer.

Thank you for meeting with me. May I ask...?

How can we help?

What would you like to accomplish today?

(Listen)

OTHER OPEN-ENDED Q EXAMPLES

What's changed since we last talked?

What concerns do you have?

Use open-ended questions on sales calls to get a discussion started. You really want to facilitate a conversation and listen **carefully** to a buyer's answers. Open-ended questions help prevent mistakes in listening.

If we can insert new behaviors and replace bad habits (mistakes), we can improve our questions, listening, and understanding of customer needs and wants.

Later, we will study crippling listening mistakes, so you can avoid these errors. You'll even see an example of how one man lost $50,000 – just because he did not listen.

If someone asks me, What is the **greatest selling skill** of all time? my answer is one word: **Qualification**. If someone asks me what **quality** a sales person needs most, my answer is **persistence**.

Combine these: **If you qualify persistently, you will succeed**.

It's time to dig deeper in **Chapter 2**, where we'll dive into into **Qualification: Our Greatest Skill**. After that we'll identify in **Chapter 3** the qualities of super communicators. I believe you will find the combination of skills and qualities to be electrifying!

Many upper level sales executives express a frustration with soft skill communication programs for sales people. The executives fear that too much focus on building relationships can diminish the hunter, aggressive mentality. **The Art of the Q** will shatter that misconception with call objectives and next-step selling examples. It is possible to do both with efficient qualification, need confirmation, counseling, and closing.

It may take scripting, practice, and deep desire to master the most advanced elements of questioning.

How much do you want it?

When Q Means Qualification

Basic qualification involves asking questions about money, authority, and need. These questions can be very direct:

What is your budget?

When will you be making the decision?

Who is involved in the decision making process?

So we build rapport, ask questions, and listen... how hard can that be? It depends on the answers that you get! Let's visit a sales case study in real estate and see how qualification is put to the test.

Case Study: Real Estate

You will hear these questions if you are in the market for a home. The real estate agent will probably ask them in a different way, of course:

Have you qualified for a loan?

When is your lease up?

Will your wife be able to visit the homes with us?

What if the answer to the first question is, "We are not approved for a mortgage." Do you still spend time with the buyers? If the lease is not up for eight months, will it slow the decision? If the buyer wants to look without their spouse, will you have to show the home not once but twice?

Chapter Summary and Review Exercise

Three basic communication skills are: breaking the ice, rapport building, and qualification.

Questions and interaction help you build relationships.

Open-ended questions like "What can we help you accomplish?" initiate discussions.

These are basic skills that can be applied in all businesses by many different types of sales people. These skills transfer from one industry and situation to the next.

Take a moment with the Review Exercise on the next page to get ready for Qualification!

REVIEW EXERCISE: QUESTIONS TO ANSWER FOR YOURSELF

What did the plumber learn about his customers?

Why did the house painter ask the same questions over and over to different people?

How did the real estate professional save time?

Questions can help you qualify buyers to save you time and help you prioritize your efforts.

Qualifying on the basis of money, authority, and time frame are fundamental elements that cut across every industry, business, and type of sales. Needs discovery is also vital!

Qualification is coming up next. Qualification will save you time, make you money, and improve your revenue generation efforts!

2

INTERMEDIATE SKILLS

Qualification: Our Greatest Skill

If someone were to ask for one skill set that crosses all business models, my answer would be **qualification**.

We sales people who perform at acceptable (to exceptional) levels find out if a buyer needs, wants, and can afford our products and services.

Many sales people waste time, effort, and commissions on unqualified buyers. Best Practice studies, observation, and my personal experience all arrive at the same conclusion: Qualifying your customers gets you where you need to go.

CORE COMPONENTS

These three building blocks build a good foundation for discussing qualification and eliminating most stalls, delays, and wasted time in selling:

Budget
Authority
Time Frame

Let's get deeper into the **structure, sequence, and subtleties** or **WHY** we ask these questions!

Budget

We'll start with Budget.

First, it is important to make sure our buyers have the financial ability to pay. It sounds simple but my prediction is that you will come to appreciate and embrace budget qualifying as fundamental.

Here are some budget (money) questions:

What budget has been established for this?

Did you have a monthly payment in mind?

How often have you been asked this question when buying a car or a house? A buyer does not always know how much it will take to invest in your products or services. We have all been asked, "What payment do you have in mind?" or, "How much did you want to spend?"

This is fine for business-to-consumer sales, but in business-to-business situations, selling requires more finesse. The budget may be shaped (e-x-p-a-n-d-e-d) and **that** is where a sales person is **very valuable to an organization**.

Case Study: A Nose for Money

My assignment is San Francisco, California, and I am already dreaming of seafood and the Golden Gate Bridge. The office equipment sales team is gathering in a conference room. My role is to step in as temporary sales manager. The current manager has just resigned and it's time for me to address the group.

When I walk into the conference room, the mood, as expected, is somber. I have a question for the group:

Who is the best sales person here?

No one answers but one young lady puts a finger on her nose and says:

"**I may not be the best sales person, but I have a nose for money. I can smell it**!"

Now I have a standard line when I think someone is pulling my leg. I usually say, "Don't kid a kidder!" This time, I decide to wait and see if this sales person is serious or just joking around.

The group assignment is to go visit a few customers. Then we'll all meet for lunch at an Oyster Bar in downtown San Francisco. The goal is to collect some success stories, get some positive energy, and meet back to share what we have learned.

Our motto for the day is, "**No Negativity**."

I ask the young lady with the nose for money if we can make some sales calls together. Going on a "Ride Along" is a great chance to observe, to learn, and to coach. The first couple of calls are routine.

Then we arrive at a skyscraper with shiny glass walls. She approaches the building directory and we enter the elevator. My sales person with the nose for money says: "**Let's go to the top**," and smiles.

When the elevator door opens, I see a stunning view of the city. With confidence and poise, the sales person walks up to the receptionist and asks to see the Managing Partner.

As we are waiting, she asks me, "**Can you smell the money**?" Actually, I really can, because our plush and opulent surroundings include leather chairs and fresh flowers. Artwork adorns the walls.

When the Managing Partner comes out, the sales person has three ways to help him make his law firm better, faster, and more profitable. Although she does not get an immediate order, she is getting close to making a sale. The customer gives her permission to do a cost comparison and efficiency study, and then we go.

We are leaving now and getting back into the elevator. "**It's the nose**," she says, laughing. I have also learned this young lady with a nose for money has many other positive qualities.

She shows belief and humor. She believes in herself enough to go into unplanned sales situations. She uses jokes to keep the mood light and fun. She also stresses benefits to keep buyers interested.

Most of all, she got permission to gather information from the key decision maker.

If you want to go to the top, then perhaps you can develop a nose for money!

Qualifying is a process, not an event.

Authority

After the first building block, Budget, the next one is Authority.

In other words, who will ultimately decide? If you sell to businesses, you will find that one person alone may not be able to sign off on the agreement. If you sell to homeowners, the ideal situation is to have an audience with BOTH spouses.

In both B2B (Business to Business) and B2C (Business to Consumer) situations, you can ask:

Who else is involved in this decision?

Sometimes you have to get someone interested to build a bridge of involvement.

The more that you move into partnership with a buyer, the faster you can bridge to the ultimate decision makers.

By asking, "**What is the decision making process**," you will hopefully uncover all the buyers including the key decision maker. Once you have crossed over the bridge to find the decision maker, be ready with questions.

Discussions with Decision Makers

If you are calling on a business owner or corporate leader, you will obviously want to do research prior to the visit. From industry publications, website analysis, press releases, and various sources, a good sales person will have some hot topic to discuss.

Imagine you have discovered that this company has planned an entirely new product line. You are calling on the President of a Division. You may want to ask some relevant, **open-ended** questions to kick-start the conversation. Why?

You are probably in front of drivers (people used to getting their way). Decision makers are often impatient, and asking questions allows leaders a chance to explain their goals. Here are some examples:

What are your organization's objectives with this exciting new product launch coming up?

What's your most important priority with this?

Even if these questions are not directly related to your products and services, they will establish an executive presence. You have to talk the **language of leaders** if you want to be part of the discussion. If you can tap into the customer's dream, sell to the vision, and integrate your offering, the chances of getting the business go up dramatically.

A decision maker can **empower movement** in his or her whole organization.

Time Frame

In the qualifying process, after Budget and Authority comes Time Frame.

The time frame in the mind of the buyer is vital in our prioritization of effort. A project that will be implemented one or two years from now is still important. However, the deal that is going to close this quarter (or this year) warrants more of your attention.

It's like when you are driving your car and you get **stuck in the mud**. What happens? The tires just spin and spin. If you are working only with clients with long-term projects, then you may get stuck in a sinkhole!

TIME FRAME QUESTIONS

Avoid getting stuck in the mud by asking:

When will a decision be made?

What is your timeline for implementing/ purchasing this type of service/ product?

This will give you the basis for **accelerating** the sales

cycle. If the expectation for a decision is established, then record that information. We all know that you want a decision earlier, but the buyer will need to also come to that conclusion.

Creating urgency throughout the buying process will help you transition to a faster and positive outcome. In the final chapters, we will review how to integrate time qualification into a Next Step implementation close.

If you miss time frame qualification, your closing percentage goes down, and so do your earnings.

Budget, Authority, and Time Frame

How do you know when to combine questions? How do you ask about the decision-making process, budget, and timing? You do that with question sequences that are conversational. It is a discussion with purpose and strategy.

Let's provide an example with a qualification sequence.

Qualification Sequence Example

Qualification Sequences will make you more money and save you more time than any other skill you ever develop.

The following set of questions is a based on **who, what, when, where, and why**.

It is scripted, practiced, and integrated so it is undetectable and natural to buyers.

Who is involved in the decision making process?
What are your top priorities?
When will a decision be made?
Where will a decision be made?

Why are you considering this investment?

Time = Life.

Therefore, waste your time and waste your life,

Or master your time and master your life![1]

- Alan Lakein

───────

I've seen a lot of sales people work with an account only to find out that the decision will be next year or will come out of another office or some centralized buying center. It pays to ask **before you overinvest (waste) your valuable selling time**.

Don't ignore long-term prospects. You can pace yourself by scheduling future meetings on a calendar.

You also may be able to **speed up** the buying cycle to get future buyers ready to buy now!

We will come back to the **core competency of qualification** later. It is not enough to have knowledge of qualification. What qualities do the super elite sales people internalize to properly execute the skills of qualification? Let's find out!

───────────────

1   http://www.brainyquote.com/quotes/quotes/a/alanlakein154658.
html#uS3SkXQWDciIh6Dm.99

3

INTERNAL QUALITIES OF SUPER COMMUNICATORS (PART 1)

Great communicators all possess certain qualities. The first two are empathy and ambition. Persistence, patience, and humor are also vital.

Knowing the difference between empathy and sympathy is a key to balancing tasks (closing) and relationships (good will).

Being patient is not stalling. It is timing the close.

We will visit all of these inner traits with stories, case studies, and examples. Unlock these qualities and you can become a super communicator!

Combine the dual qualities of

Empathy and ambition

In every sales relationship.[2]

- Brian Tracy

---

2   https://twitter.com/BrianTracy/status/349319985677615105

Empathy

The Difference between Empathy and Sympathy

My mother is a teacher with a mission to help people who cannot read or write. She went back to school to get her Master's degree.

After obtaining a teaching position at a high school, she began to teach inner-city school kids how to read. One day, when I was in middle school, I asked my mother why she wanted to teach and help folks learn.

Her reply was, "**Can you imagine what it is like to NOT be able to read**?"

I didn't know what it was like because I had been reading since the age of four or five. What I learned from her question though is powerful – I learned empathy.

My mom also used to say, "**The eyes are the windows of the soul**."

While a regular person may be looking for confused faces, a teacher is watching the eyes. A great teacher is totally absorbed in the OTHER person: the student. The eyes can tell you the emotions that people are experiencing.

Mom could read me like a cheap book. If I was ever distraught or worried, she'd say, "**What's wrong**?" and, "**Come talk to me**." Her questions were relevant, timely, and forceful because she had gotten a read from my eyes that something was going on.

Empathy is trying to see the other person's viewpoint; sympathy is feeling sorry for them. My mother showed me there is a big difference. **She would not**

allow excuses from someone who couldn't read. She was tough and demanding – always selling the benefits of reading. She was kind, warm, and feeling – but not if you were being slack. If you were lazy, there was no sympathy for someone who would not try. My mother never helped me on schoolwork and always made me look up words in a dictionary. She understood something at a very deep level.

You can empathize and walk in other's people's shoes. But you cannot sympathize, pity or allow circumstances to be an excuse. In her mind, everyone should read. Once you were a student of hers you were going to give it 100% effort.

My mother has retired from teaching, but she still sees her students around town. One night we were in a restaurant and a very large man approached our table.

"Mrs. Van Hecke, you may not remember me, but my name is Sam."

My mom rose and said, "Of course I remember you," and gave the man a hug.

He said, "If it were not for you, I would not be able to make a living. I probably would have lived a life of crime and I wouldn't have been able to raise a family." You could see the tears welling up in his eyes as he said: "Without you, I wouldn't be able to read!"

Are you glad that my mother knew the difference between empathy and sympathy? She wanted to change the world, one person at a time.

Later, we will explore getting a read on your buyers and following your hunches. Remember to practice empathy and watch the eyes! Your eyesight is a sense to embrace, in your quest for communication greatness.

Ambition

My mom could see someone's point of view, and was determined to help them move to the next level of learning. She knew where the student came from, and believed in where that person could go. Mom could monitor your progress, your energy, and your determination ... by looking at your eyes.

When she had a really great student, she called them "Bright Eyes." If you are passionate about a subject, an industry, a cause or any topic, my wish for you is this: May you be blessed with bright eyes!

Now, take that ambitious bright-eyed energy and look at other people. Consider these questions:

Can you look into their eyes?

Can you walk in their shoes?

SUMMARY OF EMPATHY AND AMBITION

The best way to influence people is to learn how to communicate. Ask them what they need and want, and try to listen with empathy. You don't need to agree with everything a buyer says. You will often have to change a buyer's mind, educate, influence, and persuade. If you combine empathy with ambition, you will take your business and sales efforts to the next level!

When you ask questions, it is a mental and emotional process. You are using your senses, too, especially sight and hearing. It is all-encompassing. Yes, it is hard work. Does that scare you off? It takes a lot of concentration and effort to hang on other people's words.

What would happen if we add in persistence?

Is it possible to develop the habit of persistence?

Persistence

Sales can be a tough business. Why do some people succeed when others fail? Is there one basic quality that a sales person needs? I think I can make a case that **persistence is a requisite internal quality** that business people **need** in order to be a success. Let's eavesdrop on a top-performing credit card sales person!

Case Study: A Persistent Credit Card Sales Person

One day in an airport, waiting to catch a flight, I was approached by a credit card sales person. Even though I said "No," she was extremely polite and she kept trying. When I complimented her on this, the sales person said that she was the top sales person, every week. I asked her what her secret was and she told me:

"It's not what you say… it's how you say it!"

Now, we've all heard this before, but she took it to an art form. Risking a missed flight, I parked my bags to observe this sales person in action. She had all of her approaches and follow-up questions ready. If someone said no, she expected it, and asked things like, "How often do you travel?"

Then she would point out benefits like how the credit card could build up points toward free flights. She smiled when she said "free" as she continued to make eye contact. The pitch changed slightly when she said, "**Your entire family will enjoy**..."

After I watched her make a sale, I said, "You are tenacious!"

She just nodded because it was true.

Nobody trips over mountains.

It is the small pebble that causes you to stumble.

Pass all the pebbles in your path and

You will find that you have crossed the mountain.

- Unknown

———

Persistence and tenacity are cousins in the human quality family. Even though this sales person refused to give up, I also observed that she also knew when to let go. As people declined her offer, she would say, "**Thank you for listening**." If we identify persistence as a quality, then politeness and tone of voice are the skills or behaviors that are involved.

The credit card sales person prepared and practiced her every behavior. Through training, trials, errors, and adjustments, her entire set of selling tools had been crafted into perfection. Her attitude was to expect resistance, and even embrace it like a dynamic tension. The momentum would turn rejection into a pleasant buying experience for the buyer.

Building the Habit of Persistence

The old saying, "**If at first you don't succeed, then try, try again**," fits professional selling to an absolute degree. Persistence can be developed, learned, and applied so often it becomes a habit. Politeness is the first step in becoming more persistent. Most of us do not want to be perceived as pushy. Saying "**May I**" and "**Thank you**" before and after our questions tempers the pushiness. Lowering our tone of voice so we do not intimidate people also takes the edge off.

Case Study from Retail: Never Give Up!

A young retail manager was training a new employee on how to sell the reward program. When I went up to the cash register, I had my question ready:

Why should I pay for a reward program when I should get it for free?

The new employee tried to answer my question but basically gave up and started to ring up my purchase. Then the manager stepped up and said, "Wait a second – do you realize that with the money you save today, the reward program practically pays for itself?"

Skeptically, I asked, "OK – can you explain that?"

The young manager used the math of selling to convince me to buy the program:

If you add up the savings, it comes to $8.00 today!

You get the card for a mere $2.00.

Imagine how many times you will come into the store – one or two times a month?

You could save $25 a month or $300 a year!

Like most sales people, I love to be sold! Yes, I signed up for the program, and the new employee got a lesson at my expense. What really impressed me was that the manager never gave up. He made another run at me after I had said, "No," and I bought. He was polite, informative, and never pushy. The combination of enthusiasm and persuasion helped change my mind. As I left the store, I heard the manager say to the new employee, "**Never give up – try to show the savings and ask again**." I smiled and thought: "That's advice every business person should follow!"

A sale is not something you pursue;

It is something that happens to you

While you are immersed

In serving your customer.

- Unknown

Upselling with Suggestions

With **Customer Based Upselling** a sales person suggests to customers that they buy additional products and services.

Let's consider how upselling is expertly accomplished an upscale women's clothing store (Hey! I have to do something while my wife shops! Why not learn a few tips?)

First, they make you feel welcomed!

They ask questions about lifestyle and upcoming social events

Accessories are suggested – never pushed on you.

They make assurances like, "**That looks so good on you!**"

They create scarcity so that you want an item:

"**Oh – that has been so popular and it's the last**

one in your size."

"This is our exclusive line, it's in very limited production."

They make Upselling Suggestions, like:

"Wouldn't this be a great gift for a friend? – Christmas is coming!"

"We have some items **on sale** ..."

Upselling is a powerful tool for the NEW types of sales people with important roles in Inside Sales (telephone) and Web Support (chat and voice over the Internet).

How can these "new school" sales people succeed? If a potential customer contacts you, you have a choice. You can just take an order and end it. Or, you can **upsell and expand the revenue opportunity**. Inside Sales and Web Support agents can use this. It all starts and ends with a customer service attitude. Consider the following:

How you meet and greet (or how you initiate the phone call).

The tone that you set; the awareness you have of their reactions.

Asking questions and suggesting add on items.

Promoting out-of-stock or limited-run products.

Chapter Summary: Internal Qualities of Super Communicators

Empathy, Ambition, and Persistence are three qualities that we can develop and turn into habits.

How do your customers view the world?

Are you ambitious and persistent?

What impact does an attitude of service have on business?

These are the internal qualities of super communicators: the elite business people who outperform the masses harness the energy of empathy, ambition, and persistence on a regular basis to SUCCEED!

If you are beginning to Q, then it's possible you'll make mistakes. Errors in listening can negatively impact relationships.

To address this, in our next section, we'll take a unique view of listening by identifying common errors we will call TRIPs.

4

LISTENING CAN BE A TRIP!

You can have good TRIPs and bad TRIPs in listening. TRIP here stands for Trust, Reciprocation, Information, and Performance. TRIP helps us quickly break down what we can gain with good listening. TRIP can also be used to assess the cost of communication mistakes. Let's look at each element in TRIP:

Trust: The Reporter

My father is a retired reporter, so I grew up listening to questions from an expert news writer. Dad also said that the best way to build rapport is to ask a person questions about their life. Here are two tested questions that most folks are comfortable answering:

What do you do for a living?

Where are you from?

This breaks the ice and gives your audience an easy topic – their occupation and their hometown. Putting salesmanship aside, this is a GREAT lesson for anyone who wishes to be a conversationalist. I have literally heard my father ask, "What do you do?" and, "Where are you from?" hundreds if not thousands of times.

It never seems insincere because my dad takes an interest in others. Dad's columns were often about real estate development in uptown Charlotte, NC. He often agreed to wait to publish a story, or talk completely off the record. This preserved the trust and protected his source.

My father, the reporter, would ask questions like:

Where is the real estate development going to be?

Who will be involved?

When can I write about it?

By not violating confidentiality, my father built relationships built on trust. Each source became someone Dad could call again and again because of the integrity of the relationship.

These questions are asked in his interviews over and over again in sequence. Dad is asking busy, successful, impatient people about the things that matter most – their business! The questions are succinct, to the point, and relevant.

This reporter never wastes time and never violates trust. The person being interviewed gives a date when it can be reported. The person opens up and confides because he believes my father. What information is vital to your career?

Are you trustworthy?

Reciprocation

The R in TRIP is Reciprocation, the, "You scratch my back, I'll scratch your back" societal norm. Reciprocation means that one kindness normally gets a return similar behavior. You can ask reciprocity queries, like:

How can I help?

What do you think needs to be done to fix this?

If you listen, then the other person may listen to you. (It does not always work out that way.) By offering to help, you are creating a momentum of kindness and consideration, which in turn can enable you both to resolve differences; talking through the issues together. The goal is to arrive at mutually beneficial agreements.

Information

The I in TRIP is Information. Listening gives you the ability to gather valuable information. Ask the necessary questions to understand your audience. Sometimes a question can be a statement to follow up like, "Tell me more," or, "Please, go on..." Nod and react to what is said, to stay engaged!

This reacting is called being responsive. People notice if you are not paying attention. It translates to disinterest or apathy. If you do not encourage folks to keep talking, you may also miss out on information that could be of value.

FEEDBACK

In the children's game called Telephone, you whisper in one person's ear a complex story filled with facts, places, and names. Each participant turns and whispers to the next until the very last person tells the story? What happens?

The entire story has changed!

People pull the information in according to their filters, experience, and interpretation. The original sender had one message; it was received and now it is different. The way to make sure that the story is consistent is to make feedback a two-way street. The sender asks questions like:

Can you give me some feedback on my ideas?

Are there some areas that I can clarify?

PARAPHRASING

The classic communication loop is sender, message, receiver, and feedback back to sender. This closes the loop. If you are a receiver and wish to join in a discussion, you may want to say...

"It sounds like I am hearing this (message)...." [Repeat the message word-for-word or paraphrase.]

When you synthesize the answers of the other person into the next question, you are communicating at a very high level. When you integrate the sender's answer into your questions you demonstrate that you are listening and responding. If you did not understand, say, "It sounds like I am hearing this." You'll get feedback with the follow up question of:

Is that what you mean?

If it is not what you heard, show humility with...

Wow – I missed that completely...please go on.

Feedback Improves Accuracy!

Even though this sounds really basic, it is amazing

how many times misunderstandings occur due to a lack of feedback. In other words, information transfer fails. You obviously do not want to repeat everything verbatim in every situation, because you'll sound like a parrot! You can re-word it slightly for a positive impact.

Use feedback on very important topics where understanding and reporting correct information is critical.

If you TRIP up on listening, it can sometimes cost you money! The following report is a real story about a man who missed out on a small fortune due to poor listening.

Performance: Poor Listening Costs Man $50,000!

The final letter in TRIP is P for Performance. "I guess I don't listen too good," Alex Perman said[3] after he realized that he did not complete a basketball-shooting contest correctly. He had to make four shots to win the competition. Alex started celebrating after making a layup, a free throw, and a HALF COURT SHOT!

The problem is, he still had one more shot to make, but he did not pay attention during the explanation.

According to USA Today reporter Mike Lopresti, the contest was at the Missouri Valley Conference Championship Game. Alex hit three of the four shots, and he still had to make the three-pointer. This lack of listening cost him $50,000!

---

3   Mike Lopresti, Student hits big shot, makes $50K gaffe, USA Today International Edition, 12 Mar 2013.

It may be an expensive lesson, but my bet is the next time Alex enters a contest, he will be "all ears."

Was there ever a time in your own life when not paying attention cost you something valuable? In communication, when you do something right, your good performance rarely gets noticed. However, when you make a mistake, your poor performance often blows up in your face. If you say the wrong thing, you may cause a misunderstanding and hurt a few feelings.

If these errors become arguments, it can impact relationships that can leave lasting damage. I'm sure we have all seen arguments that have escalated into fights or emotional estrangement. In sales, these are called LOST SALES.

I once went one month without actually saying a word. I was new to sales, and thought I'd play a game. I'd ask questions instead of making statements. Shockingly to me, my sales skyrocketed. My boss said, "**Finally, you have learned how to sell**."

Here is a reverse view: If you can't talk, it forces a person to ask questions and listen. When you listen, you avoid mistakes. Further, by avoiding mistakes, a higher number of positive relationships develop.

Seven TRIPs: Errors To Avoid

TRIP # 1: OVERREACTING

If a businessperson reacts before processing emotions, then he or she may say the wrong thing. In sales, we often overreact to a customer's sales objection. For example, many buyers have experience, and will try to diminish your belief in your product's value. If we say (react) the wrong thing loudly or in a harsh tone of voice, the message will be missed, and it will probably result in a poor outcome (lost sale or reduced commission). This is the price of our mistakes.

TRIP # 2: INTERRUPTIONS

Let people finish. Interrupting your customer is annoying. It also signals your self-serving impatience. If you interrupt, then apologize, and hope for forgiveness.

TRIP # 3 FILTERS

Filters are ears with blinders on. Our own bias impacts our understanding of the other person. Do not be a selective listener (only listening for what you want to hear).

TRIP # 4 JUDGING

Another TRIP error is thinking and feeling we are better (smarter) than others. I'm guilty of this one – the following story is about how I almost damaged a personal relationship by stereotyping.

Don't Stereotype!

In the words of my niece: "**Don't stereotype!**"

This was her response to my question: "**What can you teach me?**"

When my niece answered, "Don't stereotype," she was commenting on the adult tendency to size up her generation. Everyone seemed to judge her, and wanted to offer advice. No one was listening to her.

I'm glad I listened to my eighteen-year old niece. My next two questions for her were:

How did you get so wise?

Can you forgive me for judging you?

Then I hugged her, and said, "Sorry."

After I talked with my niece, she texted me this message:

We judge others by their behavior.

We judge ourselves by our intentions.[4]

- Ian Percy

_____

In sales, we cannot judge our buyers. We can only qualify objectively. We cannot make assumptions.

TRIP # 5: ASSUMPTIONS

You are not a mind reader. Do not think you know in advance what other people are feeling or thinking, OR what they are going to say. Later we will review getting a read on people or making guesstimates. Questions help you confirm hunches. I am not suggesting that you abandon your awareness, intuition or observational abilities. Rather, get a read, and then confirm it.

TRIP # 6 NON-STOP TALKING

A lot of sales people talk too much. STOP! I know you do not mean to. Ask more questions and de-

_____

4   http://www.searchquotes.com/quotation/We_judge_others_by_
their_behavior._We_judge_ourselves_by_our_intentions./28894/

velop a little patience. We often get this way when we get excited!

TRIP #7 JUMPING TO CONCLUSIONS

It's important to hear folks out. Ask, clarify, confirm, and listen.

If we can avoid listening mistakes and, instead, focus on other people, we will become better communicators.

Exercise: Who Is the Worst Listener You Know?

We are winding down the Intermediate Level by exploring the consequences of our behavior. How can we ask consequence questions if we are not accountable ourselves?

Picture the worst listener you know.

I have looked in the mirror and seen that person. Look in the mirror (literally, now, please) and ask yourself two questions:

What problems does this person create with poor communication and perpetual misunderstandings?

Has poor listening ever cost me business?

If you are looking at the worst listener you have ever known, then I hope it repulses you.

When I looked into the mirror and asked these questions, I saw poor behavior, and vowed to perform better. Normally we change when it hurts enough or when we **visualize what we do not want to be**. You have to **WANT** to listen. The best way to do that is to admit the **consequences** of poor communication. It's a basic matter of motivation.

It takes skill to ask good questions, and it takes discipline to maintain silence. Concentration is required to sift through and discern what is heard. So FOCUS! Imagine being able to combine motivation and observation to get a read on buyers.

Stay with **The Art of the Q** as we dive into guesstimating!

5

INTERNAL QUALITIES OF SUPER COMMUNICATORS (PART II)

A Communicator Reads People (Making Guesstimates)

I believe some communicators **can read or make educated guesses** at what other people are thinking, feeling, and processing. While empathy is a way of putting yourself in someone else's place to see their view, **guesstimating a read** is more of a system based on all of your senses, perception, and knowledge. **Questions help us confirm guesstimates**, while listening builds trust, reciprocation, information, and performance.

How do we do this all at one time? This type of focus begins with observation! Our hearing improves when we are paying attention. Consider the poker player.

Poker players often wear glasses: they know that

eyes are "tells" – signals to other players. Behind their glasses, poker players are getting a read on another player, to make decisions about the game. Like a poker player, a communicator can pick up on clues from the look in someone's eyes. They know that people may be saying one thing – and yet the eyes are contradicting the verbal message.

If you want to read signals, it means you are hungry to become an advanced communicator. To further your journey, we should visit an internal quality of super communicators – patience.

Communication Is a Real Time Concept

Real time is not the past or the present – it is NOW. One way to snap into the moment is to ask yourself questions like:

Do I wait for the entire answer?

Should I get as much information as possible?

These internal questions and answers are pivotal to our mental states of mind heading into a sales presentation. What solution set is right for this buyer?

A solution set is that mix of products and services that address a unique need or want. Staying in the Now helps you build a different solution set because you are very focused on the needs and wants of your customers.

Are you in the NOW?

Patience

Are you patient?

Forget about the past. Forget about what question to ask next. Focus on the most important person –

the one in front of you! Are you watching their face and eyes? Is there some emotion just beneath the surface?

You are far past having a script now. You are diving in, following up, discovering. With these skills come responsibilities; having to wait on answers – even if it takes time.

To do that, we must develop the habit of patience.

> *Patience is bitter,*
>
> *But its fruit is sweet.*
>
> *- Aristotle*

Exercise: Develop the Habit of Patience

How can we develop patience?

Count to ten before speaking (this helps us resist the urge to interrupt).

Physically condition your lips to control themselves!

Here is a physical way to control your lips: **Put one finger on your mouth while you count to ten**. Bite your top lip (gently) and hold it, hold it....

Let them know you are paying attention. Here's how.... **Take a deep breath, make eye contact**, and respond with a nod or silent smile.

Here is another tip....

Keep a beverage close at hand so that you can.... **drink some water** (so you cannot speak).

Patience is a quiet habit that can be developed. Suspend your own thoughts and feelings so you can focus on the other person.

How can we advance the sale to closure, and be patient at the same time?

This paradox is answered with a dual solution.

You can be BOTH task oriented and relationship oriented with QUESTIONS.

The super communicators ask questions patiently at the right time to speed the decision.

Then, the super communicator conditions their mind and body to wait for the answers.

We'll be moving soon out of the intermediate realm of communication into advanced perspectives.

Confidence and Humility

Confidence

Is a plant of

Slow growth.

- *English Proverb*

Three dimensions of the human perspective are arrogance, confidence, and humility. Arrogance is a supreme cockiness, a know-it-all attitude. Arrogance often evaporates with experience. It could be confused with basic confidence, but they are not the same thing.

Confidence and belief in one's abilities are positive attributes. The gap between confidence and arrogance can be measured by **degrees of humility**.

Arrogance becomes tamed through errors and consequences that create so much personal pain that change must occur!

You may ask, "What does this have to do with asking questions?" Well, if you think you know it all, then you probably will not ask questions.

A dash of humility means that you may not understand all the aspects of another person: Have the **confidence** to ask, and the **humility** to listen.

What are the Consequences of Arrogance?

A person who displays arrogance with no humility sees no need for change, often displaying contempt for other people. These are the "**I'm great and you're not**" people.

Sometimes this is because they are very smart or very talented. These are the hardest eggs to crack.

There is no help for a person who is arrogant and sees no need to change. This can lead to mission-critical relationship failure. **It is over until the crash; only then do the arrogant seek refuge**.

Confident people with humility can separate their behavior from their self-esteem. They identify mistakes and avoid repeating these decisions or behaviors. They understand there is always room for improvement.

A team leader with humility hires people with superior skills. It is the awareness of strengths and weaknesses that allows growth and improvement in the team.

Achiever's Frustration

Determination

Is the wake up call

To the human will.[5]

- Tony Robbins.

There are times where our communication skills do not work. Our internal super qualities are not swaying customers. There are even times when you will ask questions with confidence and listen with humility, only to be told, "No."

If this is happening frequently, you may suffer from the achiever's frustration. When this happens, ask yourself:

Why am I frustrated?

How can I channel this frustration for positive energy?

Achiever's frustration can best be described as when your expectations do not match with your results. Achiever's frustration can be damaging, or a source of determination.

To make it work for you, find a person who has done what you want to do. Watch them; seek the mentor; ask for advice. Put that fuel in your tank and double down on determination.

Moving to Advanced

We are leaving intermediate and moving into the **advanced learning section** of **The Art of the Q.**

---

5   Tony Robbins, Awaken The Giant Within, Simon and Schuster, 1991, p 265.

6

THE ACCIDENT AT FEEDBACK FREEWAY (THREE PART CASE STUDY)

Uh-Oh!

We interrupt our programming to inform you of a multiple-car accident at Feedback Freeway! We hope no one is injured.

What role will questions play?

Will interviewing (asking a sequence of questions) improve communication?

The Accident at Feedback Freeway
Part I - Police Questions

There's been a three-car collision. Luckily, no one died, but one person is injured. Police are on the scene interviewing witnesses. One of the law enforcement officers, Officer Sam Johnson, is new. He has never interviewed a witness. The senior member of the team is Corporal Amanda Thompson.

There are three witnesses to interview. Two are yelling at each other and pointing at the third person. One car is on fire. Sirens wail, as emergency vehicles arrive on the scene.

Officer Johnson has just been through training on how to interview a witness. He knows that there may be imperfect information, errors, and yes, lies. Law enforcement professionals are taught to act quickly, without bias, and with as few distractions as possible. Someone has requested an officer who speaks Spanish.

Corporal Thompson wisely splits up the witnesses so each officer can gather information. She takes out her notepad and begins asking clear questions. Here are some samples from her interview:

Can you describe in your own words what happened?

What else happened?

She is responsive with non-committal, encouraging remarks like "OK," "I see," and "Please go on..."

Officer Johnson is not doing so well. He keeps interrupting the witness. Before one explanation is complete, he's asking another question. Also, his witness is Latino, and Officer Johnson seems very suspicious.

When the two officers finish their report, Amanda asks Sam if she can provide a few tips. Sam agrees, and they go have a cup of coffee.

"Sam, we had a really bad scene out there today.

You approached the situation well at first, but I have some concerns. You have to drop the filters that get in the way of effective listening. I felt like you were a little biased against the Latino fellow."

As Sam starts to object, Amanda puts up a hand and assertively says, "Please. Hear me out."

She continues, "When you ask a question, let the witness finish. You have two ears and one mouth. Effective listening begins by keeping the ears open and the mouth closed. Even if there is silence, you have to be patient and wait for the person. I would also like to see you ask more open, thought-provoking questions. Avoid asking questions that require just a yes or no answer."

As they finish their coffee, Amanda tosses Sam a brand new notepad and suggests: "Write things down so you don't forget important details."

The Accident at Feedback Freeway
Part II - Claims Adjuster and Lawyer

After the accident, the car owners contact their insurance companies. Claims adjusters dispatch to the scene immediately to gather information. Each adjuster takes pictures. As they tap their computers, the claims adjusters ask the drivers questions and enter the answers into a database.

Who were the drivers?

What amount of damage has been done to the vehicles?

Can I get a copy of the police report?

Don Munson, one of the drivers, claims that he has whiplash. The claims adjuster looks at him skeptically, but records the information on the glass of the mobile computer.

Later, the insurance company also scans the police reports into the claims software. Now the insurance company has all the facts.

There is a ripple effect from the wreck on Feedback Freeway. The police have a data-collection process and so do the insurance companies. Each person who gathers information has a role to play.

The police report, the insurance claim, the medical record – all the information in their databases started with people asking questions.

A human being is the most effective communicator when the person asks questions, listens, and records the answers.

The information is then processed with various structured and refined tools, so the police, insurance, and medical personnel can do their jobs.

One of the drivers from the accident, Don Munson, feels like the victim in the wreck on Feedback Freeway. He wants to sue for compensation for a whiplash injury. After looking up local attorneys on the Internet, he sets up a meeting with an accident attorney who asks these questions:

What is the damage to the other vehicle?

Was your car drivable from the scene?

How did the crash occur?

What are your insurance coverage amounts?

What is the treating doctor's diagnosis?

The lawyer has a prepared list of questions. There is a method, or logic, to the way information is gathered and processed. Every answer matters.

The Accident at Feedback Freeway
Part III - Doctor

When Don Munson goes to the doctor, he faces more questions. Doctors know that diseases and ailments must be carefully assessed before diagnosis and treatment.

Many doctors and other health-care professionals use SOAP[6] as an effective questioning process to identify and define problems. SOAP is an acronym for...

Subjective
Objective
Assessment
Plan

SOAP Questions

Don Munson's doctor uses the SOAP Method to ask...

Subjective questions about the patient's complaints, symptoms, and presenting concerns.

Where does it hurt?

How often does the pain occur?

The **Objective** component includes:

---

6   http://en.wikipedia.org/wiki/SOAP_note

Vital signs and measurements, such as weight, heart rate, temperature, and blood pressure.

Results from physical examinations; normal findings and abnormalities.

Does it hurt when I do this?

The doctor pokes and prods to get a deeper understanding of the patient's issues. The patient indicates pain in the neck and shoulders.

Results from laboratory and other diagnostic tests already completed.

The doctor gathers qualitative (soft, opinion) as well as quantitative (factual, measurable) information but now needs to see what the cause of the whiplash could be. For that, we move within the mind of the diagnostician to Assessment.

As you read, can you imagine yourself doing this as a business person?

Assessment is the "A" in SOAP.

Sizing up all the factors, the doctor summarizes the patient's symptoms and formulates a diagnosis.

The doctor puts it all together and determines that Don Munson has pain, stiffness, and weakness in the arms.

Do you look for the causes of your customer's concerns?

Plan is the "P" in SOAP.

This is what the health care provider will do to treat the patient's concerns. For a sales person, this is your solution set – the combination of benefits that provides value.

The doctor decides to send Don to a physical therapist to see if exercise can help. Rest alone will not help, and massage is discouraged. The doctor's diagnosis is very important in settlements and lawsuits. All of these questions and answers are recorded in Don's medical record.

LESSON LEARNED

The Wreck at Feedback Freeway involves the police, insurance adjusters, lawyers, and doctors. Each professional asks meaningful question sequences.

Each link in the chain gathers information to create a permanent record. This documentation is as methodical and accurate as humanly possible.

Methodical questioning is also a very effective strategy in sales. If we can learn to ask a sequence of questions in various sales situations, we can learn about customer complaints, determine the causes, and uncover the pain. Then, we partner with our customers in the co-design of the plan.

∫

7

DISCOVERY: THE ART OF PROBING

Discovery (**probing**) has the advantage of being either deductive (from open to narrow) or inductive (narrow to general).

The deductive approach starts with open questions and narrows the focus gradually. If you – or your buyer – have a logical mind, you may want to ask **deductive** questions and lead a person to a conclusion.

Sweeping, broad questions require patience because the queries can sometimes seem vague. Yet, discovery Q's are often strategic, being planned and honed through practice.

The next questions often follow a theory or line of thought. Once the buyer arrives at the point, you may detect a smile (buying signal). You can also rearrange questions to adjust to different situations.

This writer Googled **situational questions** and got about 8,730,000 results. We will NOT be reviewing all that information!

I first found out about situational questions from Situational Leadership Programs led by Dr. Paul Hersey and author Ken Blanchard in the mid 1990s.[7] We learned to toggle (which direction?) in deciding whether to qualify or to conduct discovery.

If a buyer called us, we qualified with who, what, where, and when questions.

If we called the buyer to request a meeting, we asked needs-based discovery questions to create interest and desire for our products and solutions. We also set out to take business away from the competition.

Deductive Situation: New Account

You call and request a meeting with a potential new account. Your company has never done business with this particular company and it is the first time you are meeting with this executive. Here is a general discovery Q with a specific follow up:

In what areas are you satisfied with your current vendor?

What areas do you think need improvement with your current vendor?

Do you see the strategy here? You want to position your company to be a vendor they like, differentiating from the companies with low satisfaction

---

7   http://www.businessdictionary.com/article/724/
basics-of-the-situational-leadership-model/

rates. It compares and contrasts, providing the sales person with a competitive advantage heading into the decision phase of the buying process.

Discovery questions can also use the inductive method of probing.

The creative mind may start with an inductive example or idea, asking questions about possibilities. These are usually more specific (asking a question that people usually will say yes to) followed by a general Q.

Inductive Case Study: Mobile Application

You are selling a mobile application, and a company has called you. The inductive communicator starts narrow and works toward a more general position.

Inductive Questions to an Executive:

Did you know that over 50% of all Americans own Smart Phones?

What is your promotional strategy to tap into this audience?

The sequence here moves **from a specific fact** in a general direction. It **begins with a hypothetical** (not meant to be answered out loud) question that is well researched, followed by an **open question** to get the **buyer to open their mind**.

When the aim of the probe is discovery, think of an onion.

Years ago I learned that asking follow-up questions is like peeling back the layers of the onion. Layers of needs and wants need to be satisfied. Emotions and feelings need to be understood. Each question sequence takes a layer off the onion.

When a person is trained in the art of discovery, they ask questions with a point to them. Like the sweet part of a Vidalia onion, at least one thought or solution, idea or conclusion hides behind the original question. I did not think of this idea, and I do not know who gets credit for it – but the concept of digging deeper with questions works: Just think of the onion.

Discovery (probing) questions can only work when we **listen** and ask **follow-up questions**. You may find that questions help you listen better.

Further, **scripting** a sequence of strategic questions in key areas keeps the discussion focused on your industry and solution sets. Your script dives into the underlying issues and root causes, so you can introduce a plan.

Questioning and listening carefully is an ancient skill that will make you a powerful communicator. If you combine discovery with the powers of observation and assertiveness, you will see your abilities increase exponentially.

You are leaving the intermediate section of **The Art of the Q** and advancing into the ability to **SCAN**!

Observation: The Sense of Sight

SCAN is our method and it is also a metaphor. I want you to **SCAN** your environment to pick up visual clues. **SCAN** represents **S**ituation, **C**onsequence, **A**dvantage, and **N**eed. Using **SCAN** will also remind you to always be observant.

Sometimes when I say that sight is our greatest sense, the experts in Listening say, "HERESY!" But I stand by my assertion. A lot of information is out there freely. Awareness of it increases perception.

To increase your awareness of others, our surroundings and circumstances, you have to pay attention. **Focus and concentration** are required to get into a communication flow.

You're not interrogating people, or staring at them to pick up clues. You are asking questions, listening, and observing. Every detail is considered at some level. You can practice, before going into real situations, through role-plays, simulations, and games.

To increase awareness, observe details. In one-on-one communication, it's easy to observe and take in environmental clues. The obvious ones are facial expressions and reactions.

When someone is expressive, they are outwardly communicating reactions. But when a non-expressive person limits their reactions, your other senses need to pick up other clues.

Did you see the uptick of the brow or detect a change in vocal tone? See, vocal tone is a NONVERBAL signal.

For example, if someone yells, "I don't know" at you over the phone, you may think they are mad.

If you see someone say, "I don't know" while they are crying, they may be sad.

Remember, seeing is believing! To be most effective in communication, you want to be face-to-face. We do not always have that option – but when the stakes are high, go see people.

8

THE **SCAN** METHOD

To review, **SCAN** is an acronym that represents four different sets of questions, covering Situation, Consequence, Advantage, and Need. It's time to define each question set and provide examples. We'll start with basic applications and then advance to using the **SCAN** Method in counseling and closing.

Situation Questions – The **S** in **SCAN**

Asking an open-ended question about a situation gets the other person talking. It also is a path to a deeper understanding of problems. Situation questions indicate your topic, and help others follow your logic and direction. Here are a few situation questions:

What happened?
Can you describe...?
What are your challenges?
Neil Rackham wrote a book called "S.P.I.N. Selling."

The first letter is also S for situation. His second letter, P, stands for Problem Questions. "Questions which explore problems, difficulties, and dissatisfactions in areas where your product or service can help."[8] This is my issue with S.P.I.N. selling. I believe it's always wise to refer to topics as "issues" or "concerns." It's a softer way to discuss **problems** that keeps folks from getting defensive or feeling that some criticism is forthcoming. Using the word "problem" often tightens up buyers. I have also watched sales people try to learn S.P.I.N. selling. Not only was it difficult to execute, but the sales people kept saying "**problem**." Spinning an issue also became an **unpopular political metaphor** for a smooth talker who can make issues go away with made-up stories. Is that the way you want to be thought of to your customers? I would rather you model after a doctor, who looks for symptoms, causes, and offers a plan.

Consequence Questions – The **C** in **SCAN**

Consequence questions are follow-up communication tools that uncover the causes or root elements of an issue. By asking questions and listening, the sender gets the receiver to become self-aware and to verbalize unrealized concerns. Consequence questions are the hardest to master. Even when you know the skill, it takes tenacity to ask the tough questions.

These issues and concerns can probably be addressed if there is a willingness to engage in open and honest dialogue (let's listen in):

What happens if...?

---

8   http://moveahead1.wordpress.com/2008/10/07/
what-the-heck-is-spin-selling/

What do you do when...?

Does this create challenges...?

When was the last time that costs were reviewed?

An old saying in sales is, "Uncover the pain." I have also seen sales people ask, "What keeps you up at night?" You will find that some topics hit the mark and some do not. Your follow-up questions are following the interest paths of the other party. It takes a great deal of concentration to facilitate a mutual understanding of the frustrations, implications, and hidden drawbacks of a situation.

Asking consequence questions will open up the other person's mind (and heart) to new ideas. This awareness is often not enough. You need to draw people further into the conversation so they can admit there are real issues that need to be solved. Telling is not selling; getting the other person to admit the issue is the first step to wanting to seek alternative solutions. Let it be the other person's idea!

Advantage Questions – The **A** in **SCAN**

Advantage questions probe to develop Situation and Consequence topics into full-blown issues and concerns. Some of your questions will uncover pain and take root. Others will land like seeds on concrete. It takes discipline and patience to ask questions and listen. You will pull the answers in later to synthesize or propose a solution. You may want to ask, "Mind if I take a few notes?" and jot down information for later use.

Examples of Advantage Questions

What impact does this have ...?

In the long term, if this continues ...?

What effect does this have on ...?

EXAMPLE FOLLOW UP ZONES....

Budgets?

Performance?

Output?

Customer Service?

Each sequence should focus on a zone until it is either ruled in or ruled out. Like a doctor seeking a diagnosis, a great sales person keeps asking about the effects on different areas of a person's business to uncover some pain or root causes of issues that are leading to distress. If you hope to sell something, be prepared to offer some medicine in the form of **Need** questions.

Need Questions – The **N** in **SCAN**

*It's easier if you say **If**.[9]*

- Kevin Daley and Emmett Wolfe

Your earlier questions have uncovered the causes of issues. You have followed up and developed topics to imply that you may have a better way. Now it's time for Need questions. Need questions will confirm that other people are committed to addressing these concerns. It also helps to get the customer to "Imagine going ahead with a final decision."[10] Need questions will provide an outline for your solution based approach. These are fun and the easiest to accomplish:

---

9   Kevin Daley and Emmett Wolfe, Socratic Selling, McGraw-Hill Professional, 1996, p 89.

10   Daley and Wolfe, Socratic Selling, p 90.

How would it help if ...?

If there were a way to ...?

Would it be useful if ...?

Need questions establish momentum and direction in the communication process. You may be surprised at the excited reaction of your audience. I have had people say, "Quit teasing me," and, "Let's get on with it." These questions also provide an outline for your solution discussion. You don't have to talk about everything – just what people are interested in!

SCAN Case Study: Questions by Financial Planners

Investment counselors have structured information gathering tools using detailed questions. Answers are analyzed to determine which investing program is the proper solution. The following case study reveals what a veteran taught me as he prepared to enter his post-military career in the insurance business. I knew how to ask questions and he knew the ins and outs of financial planning. He asked me to help him put it together for his new career.

Financial planners ask questions about short and long term goals, retirement plans, and more. The questions are designed to help buyers visualize the future.

The answers often are poured into bar charts and graphs to show return on investment. Investors can then consider the benefits of investment by taking ACTUAL DATA and projecting future outcomes. Let's explore some examples.

Please note that **SCAN questions should address one need area at a time**. You may need supporting documentation or site sellers to help the buyer understand why you are asking these questions.

Situation

How many children do you have?

Consequence = Uncovering the Pain

Have you thought about their education?

Here is a chart that shows what the average college education will cost in ten years.

Can you imagine what it would be like to explain to your children that college is not an option?

Advantage

If there were a way to budget for this now, would you consider it?

Need

Have you ever explored a 529 plan?

Notice that one answer leads to a follow-up question. The topic of children and future education is fully discussed. Here is a **conversational SCAN** example:

What are your plans if you are disabled?

What would happen if you or your spouse lost one income?

What can we do to help you feel more protected?

What if we could design a program to help you save for your children but provide a safety net if either parent can't work?

When you ask great questions, they should flow naturally. You become a valuable partner because you took the time to **really** understand the entire picture. Questions do not just pull out facts. In the case of Financial Planners, **clients will share their dreams, family values, and emotions**.

Did you notice how the financial planner blends a collection of both logical data and emotional considerations to provoke **serious consideration**? It encourages buyers to plan before they invest. This is ethical and extremely professional.

It enables good decision-making and creates customers who refer their friends and family for years to come because someone took the time to really understand the goals of the family.

This case study for financial planners is a best practice guide for all business people. Questions can be thought through, scripted, practiced, and internalized. We will return to this case study in **Chapter 9: Need Confirmation**. It will be used to show how presentations are married to conversational needs question sequences.

Planning and Scripting Questions

Your ability to ask good questions

Cannot be left to chance.

It's imperative to determine what you will ask

Prior to meeting with prospective customers.

Plan, plan, plan.[11]

- Jill Konrath

I have often heard people object that planning questions ahead of a meeting will makes sales people become or appear robotic. The truth is that it has

---

11   Jill Konrath, SNAP Selling, Penguin, 2010, p 152.

quite the **opposite** impact. Planning allows you to focus, concentrate, and pay attention. It leads to a heightened sense of awareness.

By scripting, structuring, and practicing the art of proper questioning, you begin to ask questions that are relevant through research.

When you are new to sequence questions, one common error is to jump around between topics.

Instead, listen and ask follow-up questions in the same topic. You may find that your audience is only interested in one area or has an entirely different agenda in mind. Planning, research, and scripting questions is similar to preparing a survey to hand out to an audience. You are doing market research.

The difference is that you are surveying one person at a time on one topic at a time. Your mind has to be free from agendas to be objective. Over time, you will develop instincts on which topics are hot, relevant, and applicable.

In the Case Study coming up, the topic starts with an inductive situation question. Watch as the questions stay on the same line of thought, building a case for a larger opportunity.

How is math used to get a buyer to understand the costs of non-action? Does the sequence of questions help the buyer to design a solution?

SCAN Case Study: Computer Workstations

One trap is to only ask factual questions that limit your ability to help customers. Structuring your questions within the consequence phase can fully develop the concern in the mind of the buyer. Let's drop in on an exchange pulled from an actual selling situation in computer networking.

Situation

Ms. Johnson, how many workstations are you using now?

Consequence Sequence

Have you ever found that sometimes your staff has to wait on accessing a computer?

(Follow-up questions doing the math of selling in real time.)

How often does that happen?

> *Two to four times a week?*

> *Eight to ten times a month?*

Does that happen in other areas of the facility?

I see – how many hours a month does that require of your staff?

Advantage

Would expanding your network make more efficient use of your staff's time?

Need

How much growth should we include in the network design?

The questions are easy for the buyer to answer. We performed the math in real time. Her answers established a cost to continue status quo.

By listening to her answers and having real data in the questions, an issue is uncovered (the need to expand).

You probably also saw that quantitative (hard, factual) data can be gathered with questions like:

When?

How much?

Use hard data for cost comparisons, efficiency studies, and to show how your solution set saves money.

Organize the data in a return on investment schedule to cost-justify your proposals.

Finally, ask a question about the ultimate movement towards growth, allowing it to be the customer's idea.

To make this relevant to your world, write out some situational questions and say them out loud. This will let you test and practice before real life kicks in!

You should now be ready to adopt the **SCAN** Method in your work. To facilitate that, we move to scripting your personal **SCAN** sequence in a three-part exercise. It begins on the next page!

Exercise: Script Your Own **SCAN** Sequence

SCAN EXERCISE PART I

Here are examples of the **SCAN** Method that you can adapt to your own situation. Select a question to work with from each of the four **SCAN** components below:

Situation

What are some changes that have impacted your organization?

How have these changes affected your department?

Consequence

What would you like to see improved?

Any idea what's causing that?

Advantage

If you don't solve that, what might happen?

How does that impact your team?

Need

When do you find that ...?

How much would you save if we could ...?

SCAN EXERCISE PART II

Using the form below, write your question in each phase, or part, of the **SCAN** sequence. Fine-tune the questions to your personality. Whether you're writing by hand, or typing into a document, writing will help you remember the questions later.

After you finish Part II of this exercise, take a look at Part III, below.

Situation

_____

_____

Consequence

_____

_____

Advantage

_____

_____

Need

_____

_____

SCAN Exercise Part III: Practice!

Try recording yourself asking questions with your Smart Phone, and then watch the video.

You may want to ask a friend (or manager) to play the role of the customer, for more practice before going live.

9

NEED CONFIRMATION

Your questions, listening, and notes have saved time and provided you with an **outline** for your presentation. It's time to **summarize** points and **FRAME** the solution presentation.

You may have heard the phrase, "Tell 'em what you are going to tell 'em - - - -tell 'em, and then - - - tell 'em what you told 'em." This is slightly different:

Tell 'Em What THEY Told You!

How can they argue with themselves? By kicking off your presentation with their areas of concern (not the feature or function of your products or services) – you are keeping momentum and interest alive. More important – you are setting a buyer centric **AGENDA**.

The conceptual sales person is capable of exchanging ideas that are exciting and profitable.

Because you listened empathically – you also detected needs from subtleties or implications. These NEEDS | WANTS | CONCERNS | ISSUES (not problems) will be the agenda topics for your presentation.

Remember the Financial Planner from **Chapter 8**?

The Financial Planner is going to marry the concerns of the family to the financial solution set (products and service benefits): "In our discussion, we found out that **putting three children through college** is going to be a challenge. We also want to prepare **just in case of disability** so that the future of your family is secure." (This sets the stage for explaining the 529 Educational Investment Program and a Disability Insurance Plan).

Let's break this down as N = Need. Summarize and number the customer's N's first before getting into the presentation!

Needs + Capabilities = Solution

A presentation or demonstration that confirms needs is part of the qualification process. Communication skills that are related to presentation close the feedback loop and allow an interaction with customers to fulfill the implied promise of your qualifying efforts.

Link your solution to the needs of the buyer with NFAB-Check.

The NFAB-Check Method

"N" is for Need. You cover the customer's needs one at a time as organized before (1, 2, 3). Here is an NFAB-Check method outline with definitions:

Needs...

Hidden wants, requirements, concerns, issues of your customer.

Feature...

The capability of your product or service.

Advantage...

What it does to fix the situation.

Benefit...

What it ultimately means to the customer.

Check

Ask if the customer agrees that the capability solves the issue or provides a benefit.

Questions that Check or Verify

Once you communicated a topic, it often pays to check with the other person. If you have answered a question or explained a topic, it's a good practice to verify that the other person has absorbed the information and agrees.

Doesn't that make sense?

Wouldn't that address the situation?

These are what the great Tom Hopkins calls a tie down question.[12] (In the video cited here, Mr. Hopkins stresses not to overuse a tic down.)

That clarifies this point entirely, don't you agree?

Can we go ahead on that basis?

In the video, Mr. Hopkins, the highly effective genius, encourages sales people to practice.

---

12   http://www.candogo.com/search/insight?i=4972

In my experience, the tie down works perfectly in the presentation to confirm a must-have need. It is the moment of truth. It is time to find out if you are on target with your prescribed plan.

Watch your buyer's reactions. If they like it, smile and enjoy the moment.

If there is any confusion, apologize and back up. It is your fault – the customer is never wrong. Are you feeling the excitement too? Can you feel your earnings increasing at this very moment?

The reader must know by now that the art of questioning is ancient. I'm a sales trainer. I don't own the rights to questions, question sequences or NFAB-Check. Maybe this book is reminding you of skills that you stopped using.

My hope and prayer is that a light has come on for you, and now you are ready to transform your business.

It is time to become the sales person you were born to be. Here is my prediction: Once you embrace the reality that you will face resistance, obstacles, and stalls, you can fully actualize as a professional sales person.

One way to cause objections is to confuse customers.

NFAB-Check provides clarity and presents your solutions in an organized manner. In **Chapter 10**, we will visit the role of questions in counseling buyer doubt.

Case Study: Online Advertising

Let's imagine that you are selling online advertising. You have asked great questions and found out that the customer wants to reach a certain type of buyer in a limited geographic area. There is a budget, but the business owner is old school and very skeptical about new media. Here is a sample NFAB:

Need

I heard you say your team must have a message that penetrates a local market in affordable manner.

Feature

We can offer you a targeted package in the geographic area you want.

Advantage

This will give your business a combination of powerful online promotional tools.

Benefit

This is a greater value for you because it reaches a niche audience.

Now Check with your Buyer

Does that address your concerns about a sponsorship program that can reach your audience in the towns that you want to target?"

Note: A must-have is a golden gem. When you uncover a must-have, you have found an essential need that must be handled to do business. It is a dealbreaker in reverse. When a must-have is addressed it liberates the buyer to look at wants.

When a dealbreaker is encountered, it can end the conversation. Work around a dealbreaker by assuring the buyer that it will be eliminated.

Sample Needs Confirmation AGENDA

1. Position Industry Leadership and The Power of Your Organization

2. The Solution
>   Must-Have NFAB-Check #1
>
>   Want NFAB-Check #2
>
>   Differentiator NFAB-Check #3
>
>   (motivators, solutions, exclusives)

3. Summarize
4. Close – OR Ask for Expectations of Next Step

AGENDA BREAKDOWN:

The goal is to emerge out of the need confirmation phase with momentum. Move from a low-key conversation to excitement. Build desire by positioning your company as a leader. Marry the must-have needs to your capabilities. Cement the wants to your solution set.

Make sure your buyers know about exclusives that may not have come up in discovery. Pull it all together at the end, and ask for the business. (This is covered in depth in **Chapter 11: Closing**).

As our world becomes more electronic, we are not always face-to-face. Recently, I made a mistake on a webinar. Luckily I was able to recover.

The key to the following case study is that I was able to turn to a mentor and get feedback.

My hope is that whether you are new to sales or a veteran, you will realize that returning to fundamentals is always a factor in achieving sustained success.

Case Study: Wows, Webinars, and Whoops!

Who loves to get a WOW!? **All** sales people love to get a WOW! Sometimes, in our zest, we become too feature-function-gadget driven, and forget about involving our buyers. Yes, we get a WOW, but we might also overwhelm our audience.

At least when we are face-to-face with our customers, we can see their reactions! What happens when we are on our smart phones and computers? If we host a web meeting or webinar, **we cannot see their faces**.

On a recent webinar, this happened to me.

My headset is charged, the Internet connection is strong, and like magic, I am presenting my solution to a buyer hundreds of miles away. It is a competitive situation, so I want to show as many capabilities and exclusives as possible. In the online meeting, the buyer does say WOW a number of times.

Later that week, a fellow sales person calls to discuss this particular buyer. Because he is selling a non-competitive product, we network, share sales tips, and try to help each other succeed. He tells me that a mutual customer shared that she was overwhelmed by my products and services.

Yes, this is the same buyer that participated in the Webinar.

In the demonstration, too many applications came at the buyer in too short a period of time. Yes, I got WOWs – but at what cost? **Whoops**! I had made a basic selling mistake.

My friend provides me with vital feedback. He says that webinars are a great time saver but are very dangerous because you cannot judge the buyer's reaction. His advice is to slow down and ask questions like:

How do you see that working for you?

The risk of having experience is that we become very confident. That confidence can often lead to mistakes and we can spiral into a negative sales cycle. My friend gave feedback and helped me avoid losing an account.

I called the buyer immediately to set up a follow-up call. This time, the pace of the call was slower. The review of capabilities became interactive and customer focused. I asked questions like:

Would this help you?

Is that of interest to you? Why?

This WOW junkie had to tame the urge to show too many features. The enthusiasm is there, but tempered.

Now on webinars, I avoid the trap of talking too much.

Questions slow the pace and get the buyer involved, with focus, concentration, questions, and listening. Just because we have new technology does not mean we stop practicing the fundamentals.

If we forget this lesson, the result is **WHOOPS**!

Mistakes can cost us customers, commissions, and even careers. This career sales person just got a lesson he will not forget. Mistakes can also help us re-focus and get back to basics.

10

COUNSELING BUYER DOUBT

Counseling questions should avoid any negativity or arguments. Your tone should be easygoing and relaxed. Feel free to take the volume down and even lean back. Be sure to listen. If you have an overly aggressive tone, the buyer may feel attacked. That will lead to the buyer defending their position, and that is the last thing we want. If you are hearing the same objection over and over, it may mean that you could be prompting it by a behavior. Or is something (like deeper layers of qualification) missing in your selling?

Confessions of An Objection Handling Expert

One year into my first professional selling assignment, I wrote down every objection I had ever heard. I called several leading sales people and researched the answers to these "questions" I was getting. In my mind, these stalls, concerns, and objections were getting in the way of success. I put all of the answers on note cards. I read sales books, listened to audios, and scripted my answers. My wife even helped me by quizzing me on the note cards, and then checking my answers. Yes, I was an Objection Handling Expert! I sounded like a politician at a press conference. There was no question that I could not smoothly answer. Then, it dawned on me. I was causing most of these objections! The problem was not that I didn't know the answer. I was the problem. I found that most of the objections came from four sources and could be addressed though qualification earlier in the buying | selling process.

Four Root Sources of Objections

If we realize that there are four fundamental, or root sources of objections, we can prevent most of them.

No Need

No Hurry

Competition

Budget

If the buyer says: "**I just don't need all of these capabilities – do you have a scaled back version?**" it may mean we did not accomplish needs discovery. Also, our presentation may not have been tailored to the needs of the buyer.

Case Study: Overcoming an Objection Late in the Process

My customer, a doctor, starts the phone conversation with a declaration:

"I am not buying a new server!"

With a large expansion planned, my proposal is very aggressive. I know that this doctor is under some financial pressures to cut costs.

I simply say "O.K." I add that he will need to sign some statements saying that he knows that his system would be slow and that his network could crash. He replies that a different vendor had looked at his network and said he would be fine. "O.K." means agreement. We are not here to argue.

The doctor is concerned more about speed than any other issue.

I have a few questions:

My situation questions are:

How many locations?

How many employees?

My consequence questions are:

What will happen if three locations and all those employees have no access to information?

What is the cost of downtime in the event of failure?

The doctor goes silent. I do not speak. Finally, he says:

"I did not think about it that way."

The mental and emotional balance has shifted. The position against getting a new server has moved from a negative opinion to neutrality. It is tempting to ask for the order now, but the timing is premature.

My advantage questions are:

Would you like a system that is 37% faster than the current speed?

Are you aware that your diagnostic partners are requesting the specifications that I suggested?

Would having a better back-up system ease your mind?

He expresses deep concerns about money and how the budget for the new expansion is draining his finances.

My needs question (coupled with trial close) is:

If we can come in a little less expensive, increase the speed, and protect your data at all three locations – would you move ahead with the project?

His answer is an invitation to visit him and meet with the project leaders. I agree and we set up a **Next Step**. (We'll cover this in depth in **Chapter 11: Closing the Sale**.)

By discussing the consequences – and letting the doctor answer – he began to realize the real issues. The cost of the proposal seemed low in comparison to the drawbacks of his current system.

If we are getting "**I'd like to look around**," it may mean we did not demonstrate exclusives or qualify on competition.

If a buyer states "**I'm in no hurry**...," there is not enough scarcity or urgency established.

Now if budget is brought up – it may mean that we didn't ask about it or it may mean we are heading for an agreement. Here is the link between closing and objections. We have to counsel buyers to assure them past doubt. But we have to ask for the business to pop up the true objections. If these objections are strong, counseling skills will be needed. The main point here though is that we can weave objection prevention strategies into our sales process to help minimize buyer doubt.

Feel, Felt, Found: How It Can Backfire

Let's take a different look at the tested sales method, **Feel, Felt, Found**. We will look at why it works and how it can backfire.

If you are in a conversation, try to find out what a person is truly concerned about. The best part of feel, felt, found is the "feel" part. By trying to get a deeper understanding, you are most likely going to get a grasp of the obstacle between the buyer and closure. It is vital to listen and ask follow-up questions. If you treat this as a technique, it can backfire. The customer may 'feel' they are being pushed, rushed or handled.

Try to really understand and stay there for a while. Ask questions like:

Why is this important to you?

I may be missing something here. Help me understand.

Why do you feel this way?

The old method used to be "I know how you feel... my other customers have felt the same way and found that (answer to objection)."

The new method should be more customer-centric. Try not to rush into changing their mind or selling them on a different view.

Can you share your thoughts on this?

Are there issues or concerns that I may not have addressed today?

What would help you resolve this matter?

When the true obstacle is revealed, tell a story about another customer that went through the same nervousness about similar issues. This gives your customer assurance that others have grappled with the same issue. The success story is what others have 'found.'

Case Study: Feel, Felt, Found

My wife is driving, and I get a call from a major account. The owner of a chain of hospitals and clinics has been very frustrated with his current software. I have provided references, but he is still not ready to invest in our software.

To make matters a little more challenging, the phone call on my Smart Phone is cutting in and out because we are passing between cell towers. Here is a series of questions and answers that occurred rapidly:

Me: I'm missing something. What am I missing?

Customer: The references you gave me are not doing what we want to do.

You want to connect several hospitals across the Internet on a shared database, correct?

Yes, but we also want to process credit cards across multiple locations.

The references I gave you are not doing that?

Correct.

So I need to get you a list of references who are pro-cessing credit cards automatically across the Internet with multiple locations connected to a single database?

That would help a lot.

Why is this important to you?

There are a lot of mistakes that are costing us money. Plus, customers are getting frustrated, and the staff is very stressed over the time spent fixing mistakes.

How much is this costing you, ballpark?

I'm bleeding cash. Thousands.

How many customers are impacted?

Hundreds.

Ouch. So the staff is getting a little tense. Who is spending the most time on this?

It is not just one person. It is about three people, and they are about to mutiny (laughing).

OK. I think I understand now. This is costing you time, money, and is negatively impacting your team. You need a list of customers who have solved this issue, stat.

Correct.

The next step is to research and develop a List of References. I call the contacts at the accounts and get the facts behind each situation.

This is the "**FELT**" stage (not literally, but it fulfills the figurative role of giving the buyer **someone to relate to and get their questions answered**.)

When I called the buyer back, I said:

"**I emailed you a list of accounts with details** of each situation. All of these folks dealt with the **same issues that you are dealing with**. They found that...."

After you think or feel that you have assured, soothed, and answered the customer, then check or verify that assumption.

You have now earned the right to ask for the business. The next chapter is all about **Closing the Sale**.

11

CLOSING THE SALE

Case Study: Bob

Bob, your co-worker, is struggling. Lately Bob's sales have been awful. Bob works hard, but the opportunities keep slipping away. Bob really looks up to you. He shares the fact that he prospects, conducts decent interviews, and has fairly good presentation skills. Bob asks you to ride along with him on a sales call one day, and you notice that...

Bob lacks a **Closing Attitude**.

Bob fails to spot **Buying Signals**.

Bob's **Closing Techniques** are non-existent.

Bob turns to you with a sympathetic look and asks, **"Do you think I'll be able to succeed here?"**

What would you tell Bob? What advice would you give him? (For coaching tips on call objectives and next step closing, keep reading this chapter.)

Maintaining A Closing Attitude

I think we can all agree that Bob needs to maintain a closing attitude. But don't we all? Someone told me the other day that she uses the "assumptive close." I asked her this question:

Is that a skill or an attitude?

An opportunistic "order getter" expects the sale while an "order taker" is surprised when a sale happens.

As a friend, you teach Bob to expect success. A closing question must be easy to yes to; hard to say no to, and should prompt action.

Is that all Bob needs?

Timing the Sale

Bob may have a closing attitude but if he can't spot buying signals, then what good is he? Just kidding! Bob can learn this, right? Or is Bob lacking observation and mental acuity abilities? Is he patient... waiting for the right time to ask?

If you have a closing attitude, then you should look for buying signals, and close when the "timing is right." Now to help Bob, you get him to imagine a traffic light where a buying signal is green and means "GO." Negative body language means "stop." Then, you give Bob a few examples:

Body Language

Gestures can be questions (or possible objections). For instance, the universal sign for a question is a shoulder shrug. If you toss in a quizzical look and put both palms up in the air, it means you have a question. It really communicates confusion. Without saying a word, you are communicating. There are entire books about this, but here are some vital signals.

Think of a stoplight. If you see a negative body signal, think yellow, and slow down. You may see a red light, and want to stop and apologize. Of course, green is Go!

If a buyer wrings their hands and frowns, it suggests disappointment. Yellow Light!

If a buyer puts a hand on their chin and looks engaged, it implies that they get the idea! Green!

Facial Expressions

Shows interest – GO
Smiles – GO
Frowns – STOP
Goes Rigid – STOP

Verbal Buying Signals

Sudden Silence – GO
Asking Questions – GO

It takes an awareness of attitude, thought, and emotion to communicate clearly without words. In a way, some people would say it is like acting. If you are very genuine, however, it is the opposite of acting. It is letting people in, to see a responsive reaction. It is non-verbal feedback that can fuel conversation and build momentum in a relationship.

So there are three sides to gestures that are questions. There is the sender. There is the receiver. If you are sending, then you are making the faces and gestures. If you are receiving, then you need to observe carefully. If you do not understand the feedback, try asking:

You seem confused. Is there something I can clear up?

You look a little disappointed. What's the matter?

I saw a light come on over your head. Do you have an idea?

It is the **observation** and responsiveness that are the silent communication tools here. The questions are just an outward expression of your mental acuity and awareness. Use the **SCAN** Method's **name** as a reminder to stay observant. If you close without watching for buying signals, you may get answers that do not advance the sale.

Closing Techniques Matter

Let's get back to Bob.

Now Bob is feeling pretty good. You've got his attitude right and his timing is sharp. He promises you that he will be on the lookout for buying signals! You say, "Whoa, Bob...**Skill matters** and you are going to need some **closing techniques**."

Now about this time you begin to sense that Bob is getting overwhelmed so you decide to keep it simple. You decide to teach him to close on the next step.

The Summary Close

The Summary Close comes at the end of the presentation. You add up all the points you've made and combine them with all of the buyer's needs. Then, you simply ask them for the order.

May I write up the order?

Bob can use this when he knows the sale is made. Maybe Bob needs to be a little more assertive and apply some smart aggression.

Assertiveness and <u>Smart</u> Aggression

Being assertive is not the same as being aggressive, but they are cousins. Aggressiveness can be viewed as making an effort to win. In communication, that can also be called an argument.

Sometimes an aggressive person is viewed as pushy. Being assertive is more subtle than being overly aggressive. You can maintain a high energy and take initiative in a conversation by asking good, thoughtful questions.

> *You can be assertive by asking questions –*
>
> *Statements are more confrontational.*[13]
>
> *- Mitch McCrimmon, Ph.D.*

Yes, there are a lot of recruiters who say they want aggressive sales people. Yet, we also hear that there should be "win-win" scenarios and partnerships. Perhaps high activity sales people who are hungry for new business should be more assertive in understanding the needs and wants of their customers. This would be an example of **smart aggression**. Closing before the time is right or being pushy could

---

13   http://www.leadersdirect.com/assertiveness 02 February 2009 04:03 Mitch McCrimmon, Ph.D.

be an example of **dumb aggression**.

More importantly, we've now established that it's a good practice to end each presentation by asking for the order! If you maintain a closing attitude, watch for buying signals, and practice your closing skills, then you can expect your closing percentages (and your earnings) to rise!

Here are **six more closing options** that are **time tested**:

The Alternate Choice

The Alternate Choice close is effective because it of-fers the buyer two favorable choices.

Here is an **Alternate Choice** example:

Did you prefer the 36-Month or 48-Month Term?

The Direct Close

We would be very happy to have you as a client. Can we go ahead and get the ball rolling on getting you set up as a customer?

Indirect Minor Points

This is perfect for next step selling!

Were you leaning towards Option A or Option B?

Assumptive Trial

Let's get the paperwork started. When did you want to schedule…

Method Review: Trial Close

Sales Person: Other than yourself, who is involved in this decision?

If Buyer says: "The decision is mine" then try a Trial Close...

When are you thinking about installation?

If the buyer then says, "Early summer," then try...

Implementation Close

"Great. Well, there are about seven things that need to get accomplished:

"First, we need to do the paperwork.

"Then, we need to get a deposit."

(Assume the sale, and continue down a list of to-do's that happen before delivery.)

This is a test for **decision-making authority**.

If they stop you and say, "I'll need to run this past (person)," then you know the name of the TRUE decision maker.

TIME FRAME: WHEN?

The purpose of asking time-oriented question has three dimensions:

You need to know when the opportunity will close.

You need to create urgency to speed up the buying process.

You need to set up a **Next Step** for follow-up.

SEQUENCE YOUR QUESTIONS ALL THE WAY TO A

TRIAL CLOSE

The sales mission was simple. The product sells it-self: wine. Yes, I was coaching a sale team in the beverage distribution business. The sales people knew their industry and their products, and were very active in getting meetings with customers.

Could we develop some questions to get to closure?

Case Study: Wine Distributor

A wine distributor asks me to develop a series of questions to help the sales people on sales calls. Let's listen in on a sales call! (Notice how questions move from general to specific).

A **sales person** approaches a **restaurant owner** and asks ...

What's popular right now with the customers?
What is your current by the glass program?
How often does your wine list change?
Do you ever offer flights?
Are wine dinners ever on your list of events?

NEXT STEP TRIAL CLOSES:

Would it be helpful if we could do some training for your staff?
(Assumptive close)
Post-tasting, follow up with:

What did you think about the wines?
(LISTEN)
Do you have room for one or two more red wines on the wine list?

Can you see how questions do not have to domi-

nate? Sometimes a sequence can be very effective without too many follow up questions. It is time to visit a non-pushy way to advance the sale.

> *Follow-through is everything, not just in*
>
> *Your golf swing, but also in friendships,*
>
> *In marriages, in business and especially in sales.*[14]
>
> - Bob Burg and John David Mann

Three strategies can allow a relationship oriented sales person to adjust to different selling situations. These skills can also improve communication with sales management by constantly advancing sales deeper into the opportunity pipeline towards closure:

Call Objectives.

Following Through.

Next Step Selling.

A **Call Objective** is the **sales** goal on each sales call. Before you go into a meeting, ask yourself, "What is my call objective?"

Some Relationship Call Objectives Are:

Build Rapport.

Establish Credibility.

Qualify the Opportunity.

Identify Areas of Concern.

Some Task Oriented Call Objectives Include:

Make a Presentation to Address Buyer Concerns.

---

14   Bob Burg and John David Mann, Go-Givers Sell More, Portfolio Hardcover, 2010, p 102.

Identify Objections or Deal Breakers.

Obtain an Agreement.

Identify the **Next Step** to advance the sale.

NEXT STEPS ARE THE FOLLOW-THROUGH OF SALES

A Next Step is an action that **provides a benefit to the buyer and advances the sale**. Other sales stall, and are lost to competition. You want to **find out what the obstacles are and solve the issues** to win the business.

If you cannot win the business on this sales call, **get an agreement on the Next Step**. These next steps can go on a to-do list and take a high priority on a buyer-by-buyer basis.

You can consider this a trial close if you want to but this type of thinking may be premature (or immature). Ask yourself:

Have you earned the business?

Next Step Closing Questions

You know the times where you are feeling it and you can tell you are going to make a sale? Don't get too excited and forget to conclude your presentation. A conclusion is a great time to summarize the major advantages of your ideas...especially the ones that you could tell the buyer liked.

One of my favorite questions is to ask the buyer:

What would you like the next step to be?

Questions That Rephrase or Refocus

If you have asked a question, it may involve re-peating or making sure you have the basic concepts. This lets the other person know that you are on track with the message.

If I understand what you're saying...

To clarify my thinking...

What I hear you saying is...

Don't overuse the paraphrasing. Sometimes you just say, "Right," or, "Got it."

Paraphrasing helps when the answer is a little vague or complicated. Sometimes there are two questions, and it pays to split up the questions and answer each one separately.

If the question implies a premise that you do not agree with, you can be assertive and ask:

Possibly, the question we need to ask is...

It sounds like you are asking me...

This isolates or re-focuses the other party on the true issue, and allows you to properly address any concerns or issues.

What Close Do You Like The Most?

No or Know?

When someone says, "No," it often means they don't "know" the value of what you have to offer. Your solution could be perfect, but the other person doesn't "know it."

We have to look at the world through their eyes while being ambitious in our pursuit of business. We must be assertive but not rude.

So, if the buyer says, "No," back up, and apologize.

Ask a question or two to see what they do not "know," and close again. Have a second close that is a different style from the first attempt.

What is your second favorite close?

12

CONCLUSION

Personally, I do not want to stop. However, it is wise to just share what I feel are the KEY skills and success habits that I have observed, used, tested, taught, and verified. Let's begin to wind down.

Questions at the End of the Buying Process

Being supportive of a buyer as small decisions are made can be very helpful in achieving closure. As sales people, we tend to focus on eliminating obstacles and handling objections. If you look at it from the buyer's point of view, these may be very BIG decisions because of cost considerations or other issues. We want to reduce the tension and counsel buyers with support and patience.

QUESTION TO AGREEMENT

I know **support** and **patience** are not in the job description. We are taught to be aggressive and to close the sale. Think of **support** as, " 'No' means they **need to know** more," and re-position **patience** in your mind as a **sense of timing**. Let's look at an example to see how you can utilize questions to get to agreement:

Buyer: We are going to wait until next month to decide.

Salesperson: Of course. Whatever you want is fine with me. Why the delay?

Buyer: The funding becomes available next month.

Sales Person: That's important. Is there anything else bothering you?

Buyer: No. I think everything else is ready.

Sales Person: Would it help if we could delay invoicing until next month?

Buyer: Can we do that?

Sales Person: Sure. Let's get the paperwork in now so you are in control of installation, and we'll delay the invoicing until next month.

The buyer has a concern about being able to pay for the project. The sales person stays calm, and does not tense up. There is agreement and support with, "Of course," and, "Whatever you want is fine with me."

The questions, "Why the delay?" and, "Is there anything else that is bothering you?" probe and isolate the final concerns.

"Would it help if..." requires a little patience. Wait for the answer, and listen. After helping the buyer, now ask for the order.

We have come a long way in a short amount of time. We all know asking questions is an ancient skill. This is not the first book on the subject, nor will it be the last. This writer hopes you will retain both skills and a desire to draw on the internal qualities that you already possess like persistence, empathy, and patience.

The Ophthalmologist: A Great Wrap-Up Question

On a recent visit to my ophthalmologist, the doctor asked:

Do you have any questions?

My immediate response was...

"That's a great question! No, you answered everything, thanks!"

"Do you have any questions?" foreshadows closure. Wrap-up questions like this provide a sense of closure, and they also confirm that a person is satisfied.

So.... Do you have any questions?

If you have any questions that I have not answered about communication and how to ask questions, will you visit me at *facebook.com/salestrainer4U*? We are open to new ideas too!

The following pages contain questions that I hope you will use for a final review of The Art of the Q.

The exercise is simple: Just review the questions.

Then highlight the questions that you feel are most useful and applicable in your life.

Put them to use.

P.S. The following pages are a list of my favorite questions in selling. Use them freely, as many are ancient in origin. These are my gift to you!

In closing and in life,

Have the confidence to ask, and

The humility to listen!

- Charlie Van Hecke

The Art of the Q List of Questions

GREAT OPENING Q'S

What are you hoping to accomplish?

How can we help?

What's changed since we last talked?

What concerns do you have?

BASIC QUALIFYING Q'S

What is your budget?

Did you have a monthly payment in mind?

When will you be making the decision?

What is your timeline for implementing/ purchasing this type of service/ product?

Who else is involved in the decision making process?

What other points should we discuss before moving forward?

What areas are you satisfied with your current vendor?

What areas do you think need improvement with your current vendor?

Intermediate Q's - Means Probing with Follow-Up

What are your organization's objectives concerning this project?

What's the most important priority to you with this?

Why?

What other issues are important to you?

Q's To Ask Yourself To Help You Develop Qualities

Can you see the world through your customer's eyes?

Can you walk in your customer's shoes?

Are you persistent in your attempts to help others?

Are you ambitious with your Q's?

Are you in The NOW?

Are you patient?

Do you wait for the entire answer?

Should you get as much information as possible?

Are you avoiding Listening Mistakes?

Are you using Smart Aggression (Questions)?

Conversational Q's

What do you do for a living?

Where are you from?

Feedback Q's

Can you give me some feedback on my ideas?

Are there some areas that I can clarify?

Paraphrasing for Accuracy Q's

It sounds like I am hearing this (message).

[Repeat the message word-for-word or paraphrase.]

Is that what you mean?

SCAN: Situational Q's

What happened...?

OR a statement that is a Q like: *Can you describe in your own terms...*

[Start with symptoms, not the cause, like an M.D. asking where it hurts.]

What are your plans?

SCAN: Consequence Q's

What do you do when ... ?

How does this create challenges?

Why is this important to you?

SCAN: Advantage Q's

In the long term, if this continues ... ?

What effect does this have on ... ?

How much is THAT going to cost?

SCAN: Needs Q's

How would it help if ... ?

If there were a way to ... ?

CHECKING Q'S

How would this help you?

Why is that of interest to you?

COUNSELING Q'S

Can you share your thoughts on this?

Are there issues or concerns that I may not have addressed today?

What would help you resolve this matter?

If I understand what you're saying ...

CLOSING Q'S

When did you want to get started?

Which of the options did your prefer?

What would you like the next step to be?

What is your process for setting up a new vendor?

Are there any questions I haven't answered for you today?

∫

If you've got a favorite Q, please post it at *facebook.com/salestrainer4U* and keep the conversation going.

ABOUT THE AUTHOR

Charlie Van Hecke, fast becoming known as the Championship Coach of Sales, is driven to understand the psychology and strategy behind the entire sales process. He has worked for and consulted with companies throughout the Southeast and nationwide. As a trainer, he has an uncanny ability to recognize great potential in other people. Just like a coach helps a championship athlete, Charlie Van Hecke knows the tools and training necessary to help others succeed and reach their goals.

A corporate educator who returns to sales to test his programs, Charlie Van Hecke loves to share his experience so that others can succeed. From entry-level positions to CEO, he has been on the phone, across the desk, in the trenches, and on the front line, analyzing every angle of the challenging yet fascinating business of selling.

He currently sells for an international leader in veterinary practice management software. His previous sales experience includes training and managing national sales teams, with whom he has produced multi-million dollar annual revenues for Fortune 500 companies.

Charlie Van Hecke trains people to capture sales lightning in a bottle. He has channeled his expertise and years of award-winning sales experience into "SalesTrainer4U," his effective and affordable educational courses. From sales negotiation training to sales management training, his students learn how to develop championship-level success habits to increase their revenue and profitability.

His previous book, **Target 10 To Win!**, presents a focused method for increasing sales through a ten-minute daily practice. Now, his latest book, **The Art of the Q • Build Your Business with Questions**, introduces his readers to a wider view. Charlie Van Hecke wants his audience to understand the human side of sales.

Through targeted questions leading to prospect qualification, **The Art of the Q** explores all the interactions between salesperson and prospect that will lead to mutual success.

Charlie Van Hecke is married to Lisa, his partner and best friend. They have two beautiful children, and currently reside in Charlottesville, VA.

Keep in Touch

If you've got a favorite Q of your own, please post it at *facebook.com/salestrainer4U* — and keep the conversation going.

To schedule training opportunities and speaking engagements with Charlie, please contact the author:

Charlie Van Hecke

SalesTrainer4U

536 Pantops Center, Suite 210

Charlottesville, VA 22911 USA

charlievanhecke@gmail.com

∫